My Grandpa Had Bypass Surgery

By Penelope Dyan

Bellissima Publishing, LLC
Jamul, California
www.bellissimapublishing.com

Copyright © 2019 by Penny D. Weigand

All rights reserved. No part of this book may be
reproduced or transmitted in any form or by any means,
electronic or mechanical, including photocopying,
recording, or by any other means, or by any information or
storage retrieval system, without permission from the publisher.

ISBN 978-1-61477-400-6
First Edition

"Sometimes an apple is more than an apple!"

PENELOPE DYAN

My Grandpa Had Bypass Surgery
Bellissima Publishing, LLC

Introduction

Sometimes, when someone in your family gets sick and has to go to the hospital emergency room, it can be very scary indeed. And if that someone has to have an operation after that, things become even more scary, especially if you are a kid! This is what happened to the young hero of this book when his grandpa had to go to the emergency room, because his grandpa was having some trouble breathing, and ended up having bypass surgery!

Of course, Grandpa was in very good hands, and all went very well; and if you don't believe this, you can just ask the elephant or one of the other fun, familiar Penelope Dyan characters!

Written and illustrated by award winning author, attorney, and former teacher, Penelope Dyan, this 'learn to read' book is meant to get a kid thinking and talking and sharing about things that just might scare them, and about how even scary things that happen can turn out all right! Its extra-large print is easy on developing eyes, and its size is perfect to carry along in a kid-sized backpack! (You could even give this book as a gift!)

And there is a free music video that goes along with this book that you can find on Bellissimavideo's YouTube channel!

My Grandpa
Had Bypass Surgery

By Penelope Dyan

One day my dear sweet grandpa
got tired AND all out of breath!
And it NEARLY scared
my dear sweet grandma to death!
They went to the doctor
AND the doctor did a medical test!
And THEN the doctor said,
"You need much MORE than just a rest!"

And it appeared that the elephant did most emphatically AGREE!

AND so did the tall giraffe and the monkey that sat high up in the tall, old apple tree!

The sheep in the meadow
all of the while,
just carefully listened;
but she had a VERY worried smile.

And I can tell you right here
AND right now!
The prancing horse AGREED
right along WITH the cow
(who simply also most emphatically said)
"Your grandpa needs much MORE
than JUST a rest in a bed!

And Mom and Dad were worried
right along with Sis AND me ....
AND the tall giraffe, AND the horse,
as well as the elephant, AND the cow,
AND the monkey that sat
high up in the tall, old apple tree!

And the mermaid agreed
along with EVERY single fish swimming
in the deep, deep, deep blue sea,
when the doctor sent my grandpa
to the hospital room emergency!

And the hippopotamus agreed with this,
right along WITH the frog!

AND the cat ALSO agreed with this, AND so did the dog!

And when my grandpa went
to the hospital emergency room;
the emergency room doctor said,
"This is VERY, VERY, VERY serious!
And we will find you a bed!"

And not very long after that,
after just a day or two,
the doctors knew what they had to do!
We were all VERY nervous,
and I wanted to CRY!
But I didn't KNOW exactly why!
They took my grandpa into a room
with a VERY, VERY big light,
and they operated on my grandpa
well into the night!
And we ALL waited
for the operation to be all done,
AND all through;
and Grandma was so VERY worried
that she didn't KNOW what to DO!

But everything went VERY well,
as you can now clearly see!
And now Grandpa is picking
AND eating fruit
off of the tall, old apple tree!
Because, after all,
as my grandpa likes to SAY . . .
"An apple a day keeps the doctor away!"
And, after all, my grandpa
always KNOWS what is best,
and (besides that) he is VERY proud
of that scar on his chest!
He ALSO says his doctor knew best,
when his doctor told HIM he needed
much MORE than a rest!

"Live each day with love!"

PENELOPE DYAN

www.ingramcontent.com/pod-product-compliance
Ingram Content Group UK Ltd.
Pitfield, Milton Keynes, MK11 3LW, UK
UKHW060134240426
12048UKWH00002B/31